C000156320

#GCW

#GCW is a social phenomenon in golf. We have gone from one guy tweeting random stuff that he sees on a golf course to having the biggest golf media audience in Europe... and now on to this book.

We want this book to be a replacement to the golf socks your auntie buys you at Christmas. We want this book to be the number one read toilet book on the planet. We want you to be able to pass off jokes and quips you read in here as your own next time you are on the golf course.

In all seriousness we know people like what is in the book because much of it we have tweeted and people have loved it, that is why we have collated them all, and hopefully this will give you all some laughs!

Us golfers are a strange breed and so many of us think in the same strange way which makes the content relatable to so many of us. Show this to your non-golf-playing Mum and she'll not have a clue, but tell the guys down the golf club about the fact we all look out of plane windows for golf courses and you'll realise that for that, and indeed most of the stuff in this book, we have #AllDoneIt.

Enjoy

Ryan, Rob and Team #GCW

One
Pre round

You know you're addicted to golf when you find yourself looking out of plane windows for golf courses.

Cleaning your clubs in the kitchen sink is a Friday night tradition. But so is your mum or girlfriend going crazy about the mess. #GCW

How to warm up... 1 - Swing arms 2 - Crack back 3 - Quick fart... and you're ready to go!

I spend 80% of my day looking at golf clubs I'm never going to buy on the internet... At least if I get sacked I can play golf. #WinWin

The pre round poo is an essential ritual for all golfers.

Constantly checking various weather reports in preparation for tomorrow's round. #AllDoneIt

🐦   Trying to find a few Pro-V's in the lake ball bin at the pro shop... #AllDoneIt

🐦   I buy golf balls for a good time, not a long time #GCW

🐦   You either turn up 2 hours before you tee off for an intensive practice, or 26 seconds before you're due on the tee. But NEVER in-between.

When someone duffs their driver at the range and immediately puts it away and gets the wedge out... #AllSeenIt

The beginner at the range who forgets to put the basket under the ball dispenser before putting the toke in #AllSeenIt #NickBallsDontHelp

Yeah I'll play tomorrow... 7:32? Yeah sound, I'm not getting that pissed tonight! #GCW

🐦 You know you're addicted to golf when you have nightmares about 4 putts…

🐦 Going to American Golf and pretending you're interested in buying some clubs so you can have a play on the indoor swing monitor. #AllDoneIt

🐦 The pro this morning: "Why pay money for lessons & decent equipment then turn up in this sort of state every Sunday expecting to play well"

It's a scientific fact that anyone who plays golf on a Saturday doesn't do any work on a Friday because they are planning tomorrow's round.

Unwritten Rules of Golf: You have to use exactly 3 balls on the putting green when you have a few putts before a round. #Rules

Buying a bag of lake balls from the pro shop before the Saturday comp is the ultimate sign of no confidence. #GCW

🐦 Positive attitude, take your time focus on every shot. Until you've given up by the 7th, then just focus on the beer that's waiting for you.

🐦 Unwritten Rules of Golf 23: You must steal small pens and pencils at every given opportunity, especially when you're in IKEA. #Rules

🐦 Staying in on a a Friday night so you're not hungover for golf on Saturday... Then shooting 98 and thinking you should have got pissed.

🐦 Thinning your first chip on the practice green, ends up stone dead at the wrong hole, then chipping the rest of your balls to that hole.

My heart says Pro-V. My bank account says Top Flite.

Getting your clubs regripped and honestly believing it has improved your swing.

Unwritten Rules of Golf: A good range session is ALWAYS followed by a terrible round. #Rules

Telling yourself to play safe before the round... then hitting driver off every tee and lob wedge around every green. #AllDoneIt

Two
On the tee

🐦   Unwritten Rules of Golf 9: The first person to play on the first tee MUST say 'Have a good game lads'

🐦   Par 3 - Tee box - Heaven

🐦   Golf's Most Annoying Sayings: 1 - 'You don't want that back' 2 - 'Ah, didn't hit it' 3 - 'Don't go that far on my holidays' 4 - 'Got a spare tee mate?'

🐦 'I hit that because I thought it was sensible, not because I wanted to'

🐦 'The tee box isn't lined up with the fairway, was always going right'

🐦 If you can work out how the wind will affect you on the first tee, based on which way the arrows point on BBC weather website #TrueGolfer

🐦 When your only swing thought is 'I'm still pissed, hope I hit the ball' you know not to expect much from your round. #TrueLife

🐦 'Can I borrow a tee please mate?' #Wanker

🐦 If you've ever reminded your playing partner you get two shots on this hole, you're shit at golf! #GCW

🐦 3 words all golfers LOVE to hear... 'SHORT PAR FOUR' #GCW

🐦 Golfers Code: On the first tee: 'Ok have a good game lads!' Really Means... 'Right shut the f&!k up I'm about to tee off!!' #GCW

Golfer's Code: 'Probably worth hitting a provisional there mate' Really means... 'Reload wanker. Nobody is finding that and I'm not looking!'

Playing a few cricket shots with your driver on the first tee as you discuss how shit the England cricket team is... #AllDoneIt

The lad who won't leave the tee box until he's found his shitty, plastic 3 year old tee. "Don't worry mate, someone will hand it in" #GCW

🐦 Unwritten Rules of Golf: If your playing partner says something you didn't quite hear ALWAYS just laugh and say 'yeah'. #Rules

🐦 Nothing sets you up for a good round better than a snap hook on the first tee. #AllDoneIt

🐦 Thinning your drive about 180 and claiming you were playing for a stinger... #AllDoneIt

🐦 There is nothing more exciting in life than having wind behind you on the tee. #GCW

Golfer's Code: On the first tee: 'Ok have a good game lads!' Really Means... 'Right shut the f&!k up I'm about to tee off!!' #GCW

High handicappers that get a drive away and say 'there for nothing'. #Wankers

Unwritten Rules of Golf: You must ask 'is it safe to go' when on the tee box even through the group in front are 400 yards away. #GCW

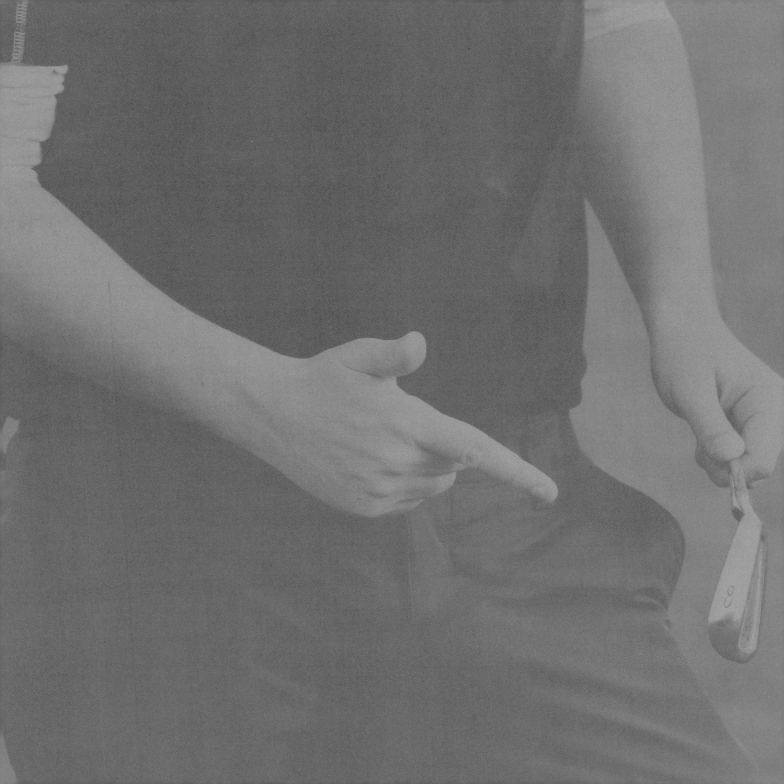

Three
On course

🐦 Finding an old shit ball in the rough, chucking it to your playing partner and saying 'you use these don't you?' #TopBanter

🐦 23 handicapper asking how you get backspin… Erm I'd concentrate on trying to hit it straight mate.

🐦 'I don't mind playing badly when the weather is nice' #AllSaidIt

🐦 The way golf works… New Pro V = Water hazard on the first hole. Shitty Top Flite = Impossible to lose #GCW

🐦 The 24 handicapper that throws a few blades of grass to test the wind before EVERY shot, but can barely get the ball in the air.

🐦 "The wind changed on my back swing"

🐦 "I was in between clubs"

🐦 "I never felt comfortable, I should have backed off"

🐦 "I can't hit my irons three quarters, it's got to be full for me"

🐦 If you can play golf without swearing you're a better man than me. #GCW

🐦 Saying 'Well out' to your mate when he fats it from a perfect fairway lie. #TopBanter

🐦 Calling your playing parter 'mate' for 18 holes because you forgot his name the second he told you. #AllDoneIt

🐦 A true #GCW is someone that tells you they hit less club than they actually did to appear a better player... "Little 8 iron"

🐦 Lost ball sayings: What you playing? - Did you get a line? - Didn't see it come down - You didnt want to find it anyway - Found a Top Flite.

🐦 Screaming 'be good' at the ball and it comes up 5 yards short of the green... "Had the line though" #GCW

🐦 Hungover Saturday Swing Thoughts: - Don't be sick - Try to make contact with the ball - Christ I'm hanging #AllDoneIt

🐦 The golfing walk of shame: Walking 260 yards back to the tee because you can't find your ball and didn't hit a provisional. #AllDoneIt

🐦 24 handicapper asking if the 200 yard marker is to the front or middle of the green…

🐦 Unwritten Rules of Golf: There are only two mindsets playing golf… 1 - Dead serious 2 - Not giving a shit …there is no in-between.

🐦 Hitting a bad shot and hearing your playing partner say… "moved your head mate" #GCW

🐦 Starting a comp with a couple of pars and immediately thinking about what you need to shoot to win… #AllDoneIt #EasyTiger

🐦 Starting treble bogey, double bogey then par and saying… "it takes me a few holes to get into it" #AllDoneIt #GCW

Four
Bunkers & greenside

🐦 Shouting "BITE!" in desperation as you thin your ball through the green!

🐦 "You should have seen the lie I had"

🐦 Blaming your second bad bunker shot on 'inconsistent' sand levels and saying.. "Just didn't know how it would come out!" #GCW

🐦 Using your foot as a rake because you're too lazy to get it from the other side of the bunker.. #GCW #AllDoneIt

🐦 Clipping your ankle with a wedge; officially the most painful thing in the world. #AllDoneIt

🐦 Shouting 'Hit the pin' in desperation after you've thinned your 60 degree through the green. #DesperateWanker #AllDoneIt

If you're not sure if it's a long putt or a delicate chip, the best thing to do is shank it... #AllDoneIt

Unwritten Rules of Golf: Anytime you try to play a 'delicate' chip shot you will thin it 60 yards through the green. #Rules #GCW

People who slowly walk off greens when they know there's a group waiting behind... #Wankers

🐦 Unwritten Rules of Golf: You must say 'well out' to a senior regardless of where his ball ends up when he makes it out the bunker. #Rules

🐦 Unwritten Rules of Golf: Whenever you chip in from around the green, you must then immediately say "I fancied that". #Rules

Five
Greens

🐦 You either drive it well, or putt well. But never both on the same day. #GolfProblems

🐦 Unwritten Rules of Golf: When your mate taps in for an 11 you MUST say "you can just enjoy your round now".

🐦 "Stupid hole this"

🐦 Unwritten Rules of Golf: All round saving birdies must be immediately followed by a double bogey. #Rules

🐦 Unwritten Rules of Golf: You MUST tell your playing partner to 'Take your time' after his misses a tap in. #Rules

🐦 "What did you make there?" - Says 5 - You write down 6 - Probably made 7 #Wanker

🐦 How's that putt finished there? - Because that's where you hit it, now mark your ball and get out the way! #GCW

🐦 Your not a real golfer until you've gone from looking at a makeable birdie to panicking over a 4 footer for bogey. #GCW

🐦 Fist pumping for bogies... #AllDoneIt

🐦 Unwritten Rules of Golf: You MUST use your thumb to flick a penny to your playing partner when lending them a ball marker. #Rules

🐦 Anyone that called their putter a 'wand'. #GCW

Six
Post round

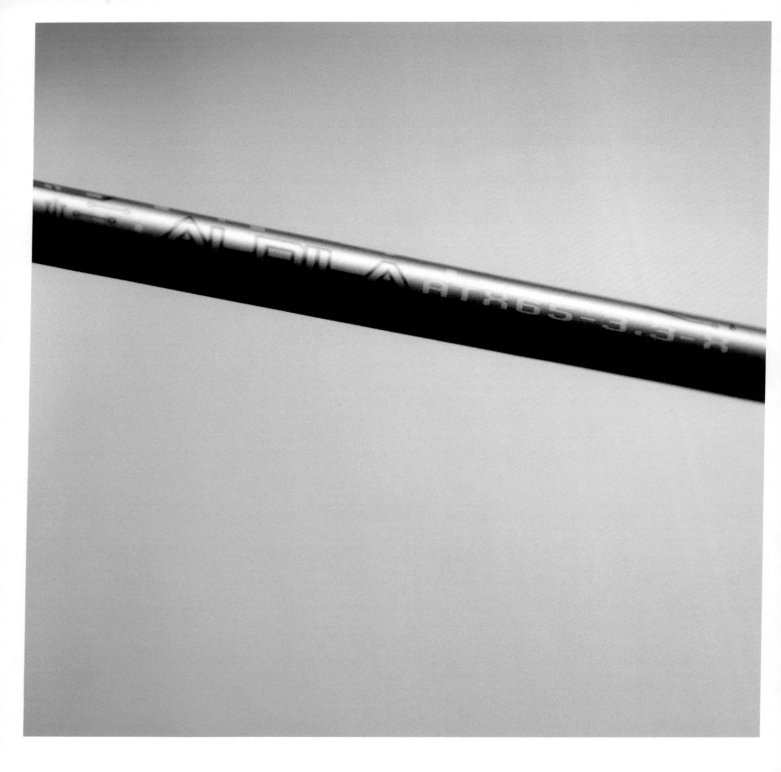

🐦 "I could be a decent golfer, I just don't have time to practice"

🐦 26 handicappers that see using anything else but an extra stiff shaft as a sign of weakness... #YouDontGetGolf

🐦 Golfer's Code: "I left a few out there today" Really means... I think I'm much better than I actually am. #GolfCode

🐦 Went on eBay after a shit round to sell my clubs. Ended up buying Pro-V lake balls and a new glove. Feeling confident about my game now.

🐦 I always stay for a beer with my playing partners, not because I'm a good lad, it's because I'm a functioning alcoholic. #GCW

🐦 The seniors that wear, what could only be described as 'Hearing aid beige' coloured trousers. #Wankers

🐦 Play a course for the first time. Play well = great course, how much is membership? Play shit = terrible course, not playing here again.

🐦 The Way Golf Works: Having a completely shit round but making birdie on the 18th so you keep coming back for more. #GCW

🐦 Average golfer who associates themselves with a specific golf brand... #TitleistMan #Wanker

🐦 How did you get on mate? "Played well, just didn't score well" #Classic

🐦 Many a handicap has been ruined over the years by women & beer. #GolfProblems

🐦 If you can hear golf balls rolling around your car boot when you go around a corner - you're a real golfer. #GCW

🐦 Every golfer has about 8 empty bottles, 2 old bananas and a half eaten Nature Valley bar in the car! #GolfProblems

Having your first drink after golf and immediately thinking 'I'm getting pissed'. #AllDoneIt

Acting surprised when you're told you've won nearest the pin, even though you've already asked every group if they got inside you.

The lad that's always telling you about the amazing round he had when he played on his own the other day...

When your playing partner is a bit of a wanker and asks if you're staying for a beer after... 'I've got to shoot straight off sorry mate'

Seven
Sayings

📢　'A Lance Armstrong'　　　Lost a couple balls then started cheating

📢　'An Oscar Pistorius'　　　A blind shot

📢　'A Holly Willoughby'　　　A bit fat, but otherwise perfect

📢　'A Paula Radcliffe'　　　Ugly, but a good runner

📢　'A Best Mate's Sister'　　Up there but you know you shouldn't be.

📢　'A Dennis Wise'　　　　Nasty little five-footer

📢	'An Autoglass'	Good chip recovery
📢	'An Adolf Hitler'	Two shots in a bunker
📢	'An Anna Kournikova'	Looked good but no result
📢	'The Condom Shot'	Safe, but just didn't feel right
📢	'The Ryanair'	Flies well but doesn't land anywhere near where you want it to

📢 'The Suarez'   Needed to bite

📢 'The OJ Simpson'   Somehow got away with it

📢 'The Ladyboy'   Looks like an easy hole but all is not what it seems

📢 'A Clark Gable'   Gone with the wind

📢 'A Yasser Arafat'   Ugly and in the sand

📢   'An Arthur Scargill'   Great strike, crap result

📢   'A Cuba'   Just needed one more revolution

📢   ''A Brazilian'   Shaved the edge

📢   ''A Gynaecologist's   Just shaves the hole
     assistant'

📢   ''A Dead sheep putt'   Still ewe

Thanks for reading

We really hope you enjoyed the book and had a laugh! It would be amazing if you could let us know what you thought of the book on social media. Firstly it will make us smile, which is nice. But secondly we aren't a massive corporate publishing house with a massive marketing budget, we rely on the #GCW community of people like us to promote our book.

So please tell your mates about it and send us your thoughts too. Whether it is your favourite tweet, a picture of you and the book or you reading a passage on a video… all will be so appreciated and we'll definitely give you some love!

Twitter - **@GCW** - Facebook - **GCW** - Instagram - **TheGCW**
Free magazine app on iTunes and Google Play

Credits

Firstly thanks to every golfer. Without you doing stupid things we would have nothing… so well done!

Secondly thanks to Simon Stevens and Adam Fowler for your design wizardry which meant the book didn't look like it was made with ClipArt. And finally big love to David Oguntona and Antoine Mélle for quality photography and all the guys at West London Golf Centre for letting us use their cracking venue.

14328117R00046

Printed in Great Britain
by Amazon.co.uk, Ltd.,
Marston Gate.